Invisible God, I'm Waiting

21 Powerful Ways to Conquer the Waiting Process

CANDICE CREAR

Charismatic Publishing, Cincinnati, OH

Copyright © 2018 by Candice Crear

All rights reserved. No part of this book may be reproduced or transmitted in any form or by any means without written permission of the author. Reviewers may quote brief passages in reviews. Neither the author nor the publisher assumes any responsibility for errors, omissions, or contrary interpretations of the subject matter herein. Any perceived slight of any individual or organizations is purely unintentional.

Brand and product names are trademarks or registered trademarks of their respective owners.

Scriptures noted (ESV) are taken from The Holy Bible, English Standard Version. Copyright © 2001 by Crossway Bibles, a publishing ministry of Good News Publishers. Scriptures noted (NKJV) are taken from the New King James Version®. Copyright © 1982 by Thomas Nelson. Used by permission. Scriptures noted (NLT) are taken from the Holy Bible, New Living Translation. Copyright © 1996, 2004, 2007, 2013 by Tyndale House Foundation. Used by permission of Tyndale House Publishers Inc., Carol Stream, Illinois 60188. All rights reserved. Scripture noted (AMP) are taken from Amplified Bible. Copyright © 2015 by The Lockman Foundation, La Habra, CA 90631. Used by permission. Scriptures noted (NIV) are taken from the Holy Bible: New International Version®. Copyright © 1973, 1978, 1984 by International Bible Society. Used by permission of Zondervan Publishing House. All rights reserved. Scriptures noted (NCV) are taken from The Holy Bible, New Century Version®. Copyright © 1987, 1988, 1991 by Thomas Nelson, Inc. All rights reserved.

Editor: Greta Barnes

Cover Design: Angie A.

Author's photo courtesy of AP2 Photography

ISBN: 978-0-9989306-1-9

LCCN: 2017905904

Printed in the United States of America

Dedication

To everyone in life's waiting room, never give up.

Acknowledgments

To all my family and friends, thank you for your continuous support.

Other Books by Candice Crear:

Invisible Dad
From Fatherless to Fearless

Table of Contents

Introduction

1. Put Away Painful Pride
2. Directive Direction
3. Praying the Right Prayer
4. Find Your Raven
5. Work Until Something Happens
6. Suffering the Test, Savoring the Testimony
7. Unmask Your Learning
8. Remove the Crack in Your Foundation
9. The Messenger is Greater than the Message
10. Obedience is Better than Sacrifice
11. Eliminate the Grace Tunnel
12. Pure Heart
13. Your Intentions Need Attention
14. Purposeful Living
15. Full with Nothing to Pour
16. Money vs. Mission
17. Cipher Invasive Visions
18. Say Nothing, Gain Nothing
19. Don't Let Your Bell Ring Over Dry Land
20. Sifting the Sitting
21. Rejuvenating Faith

About the Author

Introduction

I was waiting and waiting, and I thought the solution would come quickly, in the blink of an eye. I heard the word of God preached, and I had faith that He would change my circumstance. But He didn't. From one disappointment to the next, our requests are one and the same–HELP!

True transformation does not come from avoiding the prick that pierces your side. The most precious jewels endure the hottest fires in order to become priceless. The length of time in the fiery furnace determines whether gold is 10-, 14-, 18- or 24-karat. And even so, this metallic element still needs to cool to take a defined shape. Diamonds must be molded under pressure to be the perfect earring, pendant or ring. These pieces represent the process of life: pain, pressure, and waiting.

Instead of asking God to remove us from the fiery furnace of affliction, perhaps we should change our prayer to, "Give me strength to get through." The fiery furnace elevated Joseph to be a ruler of Egypt, made Abraham the father of many nations, called Moses into his purpose, and challenged Jacob to wrestle until he received what he was waiting for. Each went through a process that brought them from the pain to the promise. It wasn't what they were expecting that got the attention of Almighty God, but it was what they did in the waiting that specifically allowed them to exit the waiting room of life.

With the beginning and ending in mind, this entire book shows you that waiting is not easy, but it is worth it. In fact, waiting for the obscure, intangible, invisible truth is one of the hardest things you'll have to do. Everyone must walk their own path. Sometimes, it involves fear, disappointment, and failure. Other times, it involves faith, redemption, and forgiveness. All in all, the question remains, how long are you willing to wait? On the other side of being uncomfortable, worn out, and crushed under pressure is something finer than any metal, precious stone, or priceless pearls. It's something much more that can't be worn– this something is YOU!

1

Put Away Painful Pride

> *Pride goes before destruction, and a haughty spirit before a fall.*

Proverbs 16:18 English Standard Version

What are you prideful about?

My pride was my weapon to make sure no one crossed me.

The enemy was having a field day hitting me from every angle in my personal and professional life, but somehow, I felt pride would disassemble my enemies and lead them to understand who I was. I was the girl that would defend herself at all costs. I could cut you like a knife with my words and not say a single curse word. I was angry and ready, to say the least. The fatherless daughter in me was as much an independent woman as anyone else at the age of 18 years old, and you could not tell me any differently. As I say in my book, *Invisible Dad*, "I was a ticking time bomb, but I couldn't hide behind the curtain if my feet were still showing." The lack of a man protecting and sheltering me meant that I would have to be king in the jungle with the rest of the kings. I was in the Pride Lands and ready to go to battle with any and every one. That confrontational spirit would always raise its head, but God still had His hand on me.

You must go down Humbleness Road.

After graduating from Winston-Salem State University in 2007, I started my first "real" job at a financial institution.

Although it was an entry-level Senior Coordinator position, my supervisor was a Senior Vice President reporting directly to the Chief Executive Officer. God put me in a high place before I even knew what it meant. I often interacted with senior-level executives. I was only 22 years old and not mature enough to focus on my job–or anything else. Before long, I felt disappointed and unfulfilled every time I came to work. It wasn't that I didn't enjoy the work; I was full of pride and angry with the world. That residue would infiltrate my work and leave everyone contaminated. I would walk around at work like I was untouchable. My pride consumed my mind so much that I was poisoning myself. Still, I received raise after raise and promotion after promotion because God was still faithful.

Soon enough, I would be moved to a different supervisor—a Vice President—

who was only a couple of years older than me. Of course, my pride would get even worse. At one point, I was brought into her office and told to keep my mouth shut because I didn't know how to talk to people. I had confrontation after confrontation with her until I was moved back to my original supervisor. I had a chip on my shoulder. That chip would be my demise. I was already at the front of the line on my job, but I was too prideful—too haughty—to see it. I was praying and waiting for God to do something, and eventually, He would. But that something would not be what I expected…

    Pride will always leave you unsatisfied and willing to go to great lengths to get what you want, but not what you need. It will make you move from one situation to the next, carrying the same problem to and fro. In my mind, I was floating on air, or so I thought. What I truly was doing was stepping on the backs of others. Pride would lead me to a place of self- entitlement. It's a self-induced killer that would cause me to miss definitive opportunities, trade my blessings in to be ultimately broken, and lead me to eat a big slice of humble pie. In the Bible, Saul thought he could continue to be king even though it was David's turn. Peter thought that even he would not deny knowing Jesus. The Sadducees and Pharisees thought their revelation was the law of the land. These stories led to me to know one thing for sure—a hard fall will definitely come after pride.

Take Action

Remove your painful pride by being grateful every day for the good, bad, and indifferent. Gratefulness will empower your mind to always remain humble in every aspect of life.

2

Directive Direction

 *I will instruct you and teach you in the way you should go; I will counsel you with my eye upon you.*

PSALMS 32:8 ENGLISH STANDARD VERSION

Who are you listening to?

Even though I was wading in the waters of prideful disparity,  and I would eventually fall, God still favored me before the crash. I enjoyed marketing, but I would be promoted to a Retail Project Manager instead. With this role came a new extensive project that I would love even more. I would be able to travel and gain new experiences. God only continued to elevate me because I was His, not because I was conveying "good behavior." You cannot convince God that you've been good enough to receive a blessing. We've all come short of the glory. His grace is the bridge that gets us to the other side.

A colleague suggested I obtain Project Management Certification. I mentioned it to my supervisor, and she told me to do some research and tell her what I learned. As a company benefit, we could take courses and classes to enhance our knowledge and increase our skill set. After doing some digging, I found out that Xavier University, the school I was attending at the time for my Master's in Business Administration, also had a Project Management Certification class at their Leadership and Development Center. This was perfect, but there was a problem.

The deadline to submit my application and payment had passed. I called Xavier, and they graciously said that I could still get in if I acted quickly.

I immediately spoke to my manager, telling her the details of the certification, the timeframe, and the two days of work I would need to miss over the next three months. The company was pretty flexible, so this was not something that was out of the norm. After giving her all the information, instead of her being willing to proceed with the certification, she said, "Yes, let's wait until next year." No reason or explanation. I was taken aback, and I struggled with her answer.

Follow God's Direction and watch Him work.

I had a choice to make, and only twenty-four hours to make it. I could pay for the course on my own and take the time as vacation days, or I could adhere to what my boss said and wait until next year. I decided to adhere to the directive that God gave in Galatians 6:9, "Let us not become weary in doing good, for at the proper time we will reap a harvest if we do not give up." Why should I wait for something that I could do today? The investment in myself was worth far more than the result of procrastinating until next year.

The next day, I went into my boss's office and told her my decision. I said I would purchase the certification and take the six days as vacation days. Her reply was, "You don't have to pay for it, and you don't have to take the six days as vacation days. Charge the certification to your corporate credit card and let me know the days you'll be gone." I said *okay* and went back to my desk in a state of shock. She acted as if she never told me to wait until next year. There was no mention of the conversation the day before and no mention of her changing her mind.

It felt as if she had amnesia about our conversation. Something caused her not to remember. It happened so quickly that I was questioning myself. If I wasn't careful, Satan would have me thinking this situation was a coincidence. It was obvious that when I focused on doing what God had purposed, any obstacle would be defeated. I learned that the blessing is not only the gift that is given or the way that it is made, but it is also the way God makes the way. We can learn much more by the way God moves the puzzle pieces. The only thing blocking your advancement is your will to achieve it.

Take Action

What have you put off that God has deemed yours? Have you been listening to naysayers or dream killers? It is time to get back on track. You've been stagnant long enough. Write down your goal, and the steps it will take to get there. If you receive a no on the way, just know a yes is coming.

3

Praying the Right Prayer

> *Don't be anxious about anything, but in everything by prayer and supplication with thanksgiving let your requests be made known to God.*
>
> Philippians 4:6 English Standard Version

What prayer are you praying?

After studying tirelessly, I finally received my Project Management Certification from the Xavier Leadership and Development Center, and I graduated from Xavier University with an MBA. I was ready for what's next. I liked the project I had, but with my degree, I thought I was entitled to be held to a higher standard and included in additional strategic assignments. With my pride in the way, and my mind made up, I prayed a prayer that would not help me in the waiting room of life—it only prolonged my trip.

My misunderstanding of God caused me to constantly pray, "God, please get me out of this job!" I would put in multiple applications every week just hoping something would bite. I'd have interviews, and never get hired. This happened for almost a year. What I thought was happenstance, was actually being blocked by God. My job paid for my Graduate Degree and Project Management Certification. If I were to quit the job before two years, I would have to reimburse the payment immediately. Of course, I didn't have the money to pay anyone back anything, but being the haughty person I was, I did not care about the rules—I just wanted out.

One day, I was in the office looking through my supervisor's email. I was given access when I was first hired, but this time I was being nosey. I scrolled through the emails and stumbled upon a list of employees that were going to be laid off. I was looking at the long list of high positions with their pay listed beside their names. I scrolled slowly. I knew all of them. I kept scrolling, only to find my name at the bottom of the list. Not only was I in shock, but I was furious. It would take at least a month for them to start laying people off. One by one, they were gone. Soon enough, it was my turn. Sitting on this information with no way out was devastating. I was watching the end flash in front of my eyes, and the only being that could do something—God—wouldn't.

Well, I got what I wanted. It just wasn't the way I wanted it. I was laid off in January, 2011. I was too disappointed to see the good in the situation. How could God allow them to get rid of me when they treated me like this? I was His child, so how dare He allow this to happen to His child? I looked at the situation and thought, *God, You did not win this one!* I missed the blessing of $40,000 of free schooling, and I displayed a lack of maturity and a selfish demeanor. God did not do it the way I had anticipated, but He did what I asked of Him. To my own demise, I prayed the wrong prayer. I prayed "Help me get out," instead of "Help me get through."

Pray God's will be done.

The art of prayer is not pretentious or significant. It's the heart of the person praying that vastly changes the innermost sanctum of the heavenlies. As God's people, we want a higher calling, but the process requires that our selfish ways be crushed and broken. How can we seek the greatness of God if our constant prayer is to get out of the fiery furnace of affliction? Just as a teacher gives a student a test to see how much they've learned, God allows us to be tried. In turn, we beg the "teacher" to take the test from us. In the classroom, that would cause us to fail. This is also true in the spiritual realm. We never pass to the next level because we refuse to do what is required at *this* level. There are no "free" passes. Eventually, you must pass the test.

Take Action

Pray the prayer of faith. Jesus prayed, "... let this cup pass from me; nevertheless, not as I will, but as you will." Trust God that the situation will develop your character and transform your life.

4

Find Your Raven

 *Consider the ravens: they neither sow nor reap, they have neither storehouse nor barn, and yet God feeds them. Of how much value are you than the birds!*

Luke 12:24 English Standard Version

Where's your raven?

Waiting on God for a very long time could potentially make anyone lose their faith

if they do not truly believe in His promises. After being laid off, I sunk into misery. I was mad at my employer, mad at myself, and most of all mad at God for putting me in this situation in the first place. This job was supposed to be my blessing, but it ended up being my curse, or so I thought. Every day I would ignore God. Even on Sundays, I would go to church and have nothing to say to Him. I thought paying tithes and offering was enough for Him to look out for me. I thought this was some type of deal, and when I was left high and dry, I presumed He failed.

But did He fail? Or was my failure my fault? I was pointing the finger at Him, but I had four fingers pointing back at me. Everyone should be humble enough to accept the lessons of life and choose to be thankful for the life they are living. I was neither. Even though my hope was desolate, and I couldn't see my way out, God always had a raven for me.

Throughout God's word, you'll find that ravens are not only a sign of life, but they are on assignment from God. The raven would show Noah and his family that the flooding of God's wrath was over–they could now walk on dry land. In 1 Kings 17:4, God says, "You will drink from the brook, and I have directed the ravens to supply you with food there." Yet, at other times, the ravens were regarded as great birds that God provided for when they called. Ravens were blessings, and if I were to survive in this desert, I would need to find my raven.

Ravens are God's blessings.

Government financial assistance via unemployment was not enough to cover my bills. My car payment would require all the money, leaving me nothing for rent, food, utilities, cell phone, etc. I never stopped giving my tithes and offering. In fact, I gave even more. I had to move back in with my mom to make ends meet but I really wasn't making ends meet, God was. My mom would provide food, shelter, and a host of other things. My eyes were so focused on the situation that I could not see that God had provided a raven. I was a bird eating the crumbs along the bread trail until one day when I found the loaf.

After five months of looking for a job, I finally landed a temporary contract role making more money than I made before the layoff. That was a raven moment. God will bless you with more, even when your qualifications leave you deserving less. Just three months later, my assignment would end. Although I was right back in the situation of lack, my raven had led me to a sign of life. The role would boost my confidence and show me that God was in control.

God said that if He'll take care of the raven, then why wouldn't He take care of me? I had gotten myself into this predicament in the first place. It would be difficult to recover, but reality would be too evident to overlook. I was more valuable than the raven, and God would look after His own.

Take Action

If you are in a place of lack, do not be discouraged. Find your raven. Whether it's a person or a place, the raven is there to show you that God is not through with you yet. It is only the beginning.

5

Work Until Something Happens

> *Whatever you do, work at it with all your heart, as working for the Lord, not for human masters, since you know that you will receive an inheritance from the Lord as a reward. It is the Lord Christ you are serving.*

COLOSSIANS 3:23–24 NEW INTERNATIONAL VERSION

Have you stopped working?

Work—a state that some people dread, and some people dream of.

The younger you are, the more you hope to enter the workforce and change your life. The older you get, the more annoyed you become with co-workers, pay, authority, and business. Tragically, we gradually change from being grateful to being ungrateful. And to our detriment, our short-term experience has become interwoven with long-term side effects. Our tunnel vision has cost us our happiness.

After being laid off again, I did not know what to do. I was back in the waiting room of life again wondering how I got back so fast. I had nothing but space and opportunity, but I needed to continue to move forward. I continued to apply for jobs, but I would only get to the second round of interviews. I refused to stay at home and do nothing. I finally decided to start volunteering to clean the church I attended. I chose to keep working. If I would take care of God's house, I knew He would take care of mine.

Cleaning the church was a humbling experience for me. Very few people knew I was cleaning the church, and the congregation certainly didn't know that I was preserving the space for them to have a clean worship environment. I was standing in the waiting room of life. God was teaching me that trying to escape the waiting room, without taking the proper steps to understand would only lead me to another failed test. I had to keep the big picture next to my heart.

Keep working.

Jesus came to earth to do one thing only—to serve. God is a gracious God, and of course, Jesus was blessed, but His primary objective was to serve other people. Why isn't our primary objective the same? Our focus should be to search out who God has called us to help, and to be a blessing to that person. While we're in that place of servitude, we quickly learn that God has something for us to learn. He'll show us the mirror of reflection so we can recognize and change some attributes that are not fit for our next phase of life. Many people face the same challenge. They are stuck in their tracks waiting for the next blessing to come along like a tornado and overtake them. Those same people are sitting in the waiting room of life until they shift their mindset. They're not in the waiting room to enhance their wealth. They don't need to stop what they're doing, but to continue their drive. A blessing may not be a stranger giving you $10,000, a stranger paying off your student loans, or a passerby giving you a new house. This is life; and even though those blessings are possible and have happened, the most important question to ask is: *Why did God send me here?* Then you need to work until something happens.

Take Action

Look beyond the four walls of the place you're in, and stretch your mind toward the greater calling. Whether you're volunteering daily or going to work, your mission is to be of service. Ask God daily for an encounter with someone that you can help.

6

Suffering the Test, Savoring the Testimony

> *And they overcame and conquered him because of the blood of the Lamb and because of the word of their testimony, for they did not love their life and renounce their faith even when they faced death.*
>
> REVELATION 12:11 AMPLIFIED VERSION

Have you shared your testimony?

God humbled me and corrected my prayer, all while sending me a raven.

Even though I was being transformed through a process that would make me a better person, the truth was I had yet to pass the test. As I previously stated, one way or another, you must pass the test. I would be tried again, but not until I was wise enough and humble enough to learn the lesson God wanted to teach me. Until then, I would be broke, miserable, and mad at God.

Being mad at God showed me that it is possible to falsely accuse a loved one of failing you, when it's you that may need the lesson. I needed to grasp who God was in my life and why His direction was to lead me to take a path I'd never taken. He had great plans for me, but He could not take me to the next level until I learned to be who He had called me to be. Growth pains were being inflicted, but I couldn't see God's plan unless I took the responsibility to look for it.

After two years without a steady job, I finally landed a full-time marketing position in Greensboro, North Carolina. Although it was a seven-hour distance from my home in Dayton, Ohio, I had gone to undergraduate school in North Carolina, so I was familiar with the area. I was extremely happy to be back. I had suffered for fourteen months, which seemed never ending. This was a very small company and a brand new position. With this new role, came new hurdles. My position was to introduce new advertising processes and procedures to ensure all of the marketing was cohesive and cost productive. In addition, I would design new marketing programs, including collateral. Multiple offices undertook marketing on their own, which left the company disjointed. It was a challenge, but I thought it was going okay.

Other employees had a different opinion, and they expressed it to senior leadership. After looking at where the company was going, they did not think having a new position at this time was in their best interest. The employees did not want change, and they were not willing to implement it. Often when change occurs, people are resistant. My boss brought me into an office and gave me the news. Though no fault of my own, I was receiving an unexpected blow. Without senior leaders supporting the outlook of the new position, it would lead me back to a familiar place—the waiting room of life. I had just started in March—moved seven hours away—and after four months I was being laid off, again.

This was the same test I had seen before. This time I was determined to pass. It was shocking to say the least, but I learned early on that I couldn't depend on a job to be my source. The job was only a resource. I told God, "I believe that You are working things out for me. I trust that You will supply all my needs." By the next day, my aunt sent me an announcement of a marketing position in my hometown of Dayton, Ohio. I applied and quickly received a call back. Within a week, after a couple of interviews, I was hired. With this promotion, I made $10,000 more a year than I made at the marketing position in North Carolina.

Let me recap: I failed God's first test. I was laid off and mad at God because I felt a sense of entitlement and leaned on God as if He was my "doer." I passed the second test. I was laid off a second time, and yet I humbled myself and graciously depended on God to set the path before me. He had taken care of me all this time, and I knew if He did it before, He could do it again. The first time I failed, it took me fourteen months to recover because my response in the waiting room was prideful and haughty. The second time, I passed the test and received a job opportunity in seven days because my response in the waiting room was humbleness and patience.

You're going to get a testimony out of this.

The evidence is real. You can choose how long it will take you to pass the test. It can take years, or it can take days. It's all up to you. There are no shortcuts, but what you learn and how you respond will activate your exit. Not until I passed the test did I receive the key to exiting the waiting room of life. I finally had permission to move to the next level. I suffered the test; now I can tell you the testimony.

Take Action

Are you suffering through a time of trial? Expand your mind to see what God is challenging you to do. You must pass the test, or you will experience it again. Examine yourself today. What do you need to do to get to the next level? What will be your testimony?

7

Unmask Your Learning

> *If anyone imagines that he knows something, he does not yet know as he ought to know.*
>
> 1 Corinthians 8:2 English Standard Version

Have you unmasked your learning?

As we grow, we are infused with learnings and traditions of man

that monopolize our minds and hearts. From infancy to adulthood, we search for the truth only to receive masked learning. We have learned generational curses, stereotypes, and ungodly traditions that we continue to pass on to our children. We learn different ways to handle life's storms, and yet we operate in one world. From generation to generation, troubling ideas and inaccurate directions are given by society, family members, and friends as a guide to travel the path of life. We fail to guard our ears and our hearts, so we're led to masked learning.

Our hope is in the future, but the present is a reflection of our unhealed past. We have been open to teachings from our ancestors whether good, bad, or indifferent. The lack of wisdom and torn character warped us into a state of insurgency that has yet to change our present and our future. We are fragmented into a cluster of tragic indifference.

From early adolescence, parents raise their children to "Do what I say," not "Do what I do." The lack of an example and inadequate knowledge has led to adults who lack the power of self-worth and are incapable of self-reflection and accurate self-direction. We are raising a society that refuses to take responsibility for ourselves, let alone the sufferings of the next generation.

The angry adults are teaching anger. The vengeful are teaching revenge. The emotionless are teaching to stifle emotions. Rapists are teaching how to rape. The fatherless are teaching their sons to be fatherless and their daughters to raise fatherless children. The fearful are teaching never to have faith. The strong are teaching never to depend on God. When will it end?

Broken hearts and unhealed pain leads to masked learning.

Change starts with one individual. What's clearly defined doesn't have to be explained, but sometimes what's learned must be negated. Fight for yourself. Fight for the next generation. Refuse to let anything wrong you've learned over the years be imbedded in your life and leave an ambiguous mark. Hit the reset button. Reset does not take you back to your previous state; it takes you back to your original state. Your original state as God's child means that you were made in His image. Everything that you've learned, you'll need to reevaluate through God's principles, and you must examine and perhaps unlearn what you think you know. It's time to take the mask off and expose and embrace the truth.

Take Action

Remove the mask. Read the Bible and evaluate where your beliefs need to change. Ask God for wisdom and knowledge to understand the truth and to alter your way of retaining generations of masked learning.

8

Remove the Crack in Your Foundation

 *Therefore, if anyone is in Christ, he is a new creation. The old has passed away; behold, the new has come.*

2 Corinthians 5:17 English Standard Version

Where's the crack in your foundation?

Foundations are as strong as the ground they're built on.

If the ground moves, so will the foundation. Just think! A new home can end up with cracks, ridges, and leaks if the foundation is laid incorrectly. With water coming in and cracks surfacing, the owner of the home would need to pursue immediate resolution. Depending on the correction that is necessary, it would result in stripping down to the home's core—its foundation.

Let's relate this lesson to life. God is our foundation, and we are the ground.

With Him, we are built high and looked upon as a house of His inheritance. His craftsmanship has made us a masterpiece in His eyes. If God is the foundation of our hearts, then how could there be a crack? The crack leads to one question: did we settle properly, or did we shift during life's storm? The key is that the foundation did not change the ground– the ground changed and shifted the foundation.

Stop settling.

We've settled continuously for life's disappointment, discouragement, brokenness, and torment. Instead of standing in the truth of God's word and His promises, we've shifted to engage and accept our circumstances. The crack is not only from masked learning; the crack is also what we've built on the foundation of our hearts, in addition to mixing in a little of God. The weight of our past that we continue to carry has broken the carrier. Settling for less than we should only leaves us to mope around, thereby displacing our feelings. The crack apparently shows that what we need is to relieve the weight and refresh the foundation.

This is your foundation, and there's work to do. If anyone should want change, it should be you. But, let me be clear, God will not steady the crack in your foundation. If He did, the residue of the fix would be seen. Instead of repairing, He replaces. God makes all things new. The refreshing overcast of His love and the sensitive guidance of the Holy Spirit will penetrate your heart and remove the unsteadiness of your foundation. You will now stand on holy ground. Are you willing to take the first step?

Take Action

As you measure the crack in your foundation—whether big or small— it must be fixed. With a leak in your foundation, anything can get in. Ask God to replace your foundation with wholeness today.

9

The Messenger is Greater than the Message

Jesus answered her, "if you knew the gift of God and who it is that is saying to you 'Give me drink,' you would have asked Him and He would have given you living water.

JOHN 4:10 ENGLISH STANDARD VERSION

Have you had your encounter with the messenger?

The testimonies of God's miracles and the work of our salvation

through Jesus Christ make us stronger in our daily race of living. However, we continue—to no avail—only to be led by the works of a testimony that is not our own. We must have our own testimony regarding God, the Messenger. The resolution is to have a personal relationship with Him and understand who He truly is in our lives. We cannot continue to be handed a testimony, yet have no knowledge of how God truly works in us.

In the Bible, there is a compelling story of the woman at the well. It captivates the prevailing truth that there's no substitute for meeting Jesus Christ. On the way to Galilee, Jesus explains in John 4:4 that He had to go through Samaria. Many Jews chose another route because of the discourse between the Jews and Samaritans. If Jesus, being a Jew, had to go through Samaria, it was for one reason: to meet the woman at the well. Before meeting her, Jesus would first tell the disciples to get food. Notice that Jesus must have this conversation with her alone. He dismissed the disciples on purpose. This encounter would not be a show, nor would it warrant everyone knowing her past and her present.

Her encounter with Jesus Christ would change her life forever, but she first had to move past the message for her to realize the Messenger was right in front of her. Throughout the beginning of the fourth chapter of John, Jesus draws her into conversation by removing the traditions of men, and bringing to life the stories she'd been told about the coming of Jesus Christ. While in dialog, she asks Jesus if He is greater than her ancestor, Jacob. She even mentions that Jacob left an inheritance and worshipped. The stories were obviously carried down from generation to generation, and still, the value of the message clouded her judgment. The stories overshadowed the truth, as if she could take the testimonies of her forefathers and seal them as her own.

Jesus would have further dialog about the spiritual well that would never run dry and reveal her current and past relationship status. Still, she did not know who she was talking to. Not until she talked about believing in Jesus Christ did the conversation change. Previously, she had talked about the traditions of men, but I believe God was waiting for her to confess her belief in the unseen – Jesus Christ. When Jesus confessed that He was the Messiah, then she ran off to tell the whole town about her encounter.

His word. The incredible reality is that the message is still not greater than the Messenger. This woman was told about Jesus her whole life, but her reaction to the message would not be the same as her encounter with the Messenger.

Don't settle for the message.

Her testimony would cause many to believe, but the town needed to have their own experience with Jesus. John 4:42–43 states, "They said to the woman, "It is no longer because of what you said that we believe, for we have heard for ourselves, and we know that this is indeed the Savior of the world." And many more believed because of

Take Action

Although testimonies help us to overcome, we must have our own testimony. Being aware of who God is will never equate to knowing God for yourself. Today, ask the Holy Spirit to show you who God is in your life. You'll have a first-hand encounter you'll never forget.

10

Obedience is Better than Sacrifice

> *Does the Lord delight in burnt offerings and sacrifices, as much as in obeying the Lord? To obey is better than sacrifice, and to heed is better than the fat of rams.*
>
> 1 Samuel 15:22 New International Version

Who are you obeying?

Sacrificing is a standard of living in God.

Everyone that is known as mighty has had to sacrifice something to maximize their life and be prudent for God's kingdom. One thing I have learned is that when you sacrifice, you always give out of what you have. Jesus says, "Give and it will be given back to you." Faith is not needed to give; it is only needed to receive your blessing for giving.

Many people will give freely since the Bible guides them to do so. This was me. Whether it was clothes, time, or money, I was just fine with sharing because I knew the principle of receiving was simple: *I'll get it back in good measure, pressed down, shaken together, and running over.* I tested this principle over and over again, and God proved it to be true. I gave as long as I was not embarrassed when doing so. I would remain guarded in the place of inauthenticity to fit in with the world, and at the same time, I would beg God to use me for His glory. I didn't understand that being used meant not only being sacrificial, but being obedient.

Sacrificing is good, but it also can make you think that you're the hero. If you are not humble enough to give God the glory that He's due, you'll think that the principle is the recourse of your action and not His promise. Even though I thought my sacrifice was out of love, it was out of my tradition. That's why obedience is critical. Sacrifice can be done in the dark, but obedience must be done in the light. You only obey those whom you love. Not walking in obedience with God and using my authority would buy me a one-way ticket to the waiting room of life. I could not grow in God until I inclined my ear to hear His voice. I needed to understand that His love was everlasting, and realize that He provides a way and preserves me when He calls me to action.

> If you love God, then do what He says.

Society's judgment may bear down on you when you try to obey God. That's an illusion that Satan shows us. However, it should never be bigger than the mission that God has given us. Someone is waiting on our obedience. If we're ever going to stand up and change this world, we must be willing to act. God is looking for people that will stand on His word, advance the kingdom despite the circumstance, and trust that He will not leave us.

Obedience will always be better than sacrifice, but you must do both. Sacrifice takes from what exists, but obedience creates what does not exist. Sacrifice opens the door, while obedience creates a new path. The underlying goal of following God's lead is the same whether you obey or sacrifice, but each approach develops different strengths that will take you to new levels. If you want the anointing, choose to pursue both today.

Take Action

Release your control, and place God on the throne of your life. Obey and sacrifice as He leads you. Although it may not feel comfortable, it will work out for your good and to His glory.

11

Eliminate the Grace Tunnel

> *And since it is through God's kindness, then it is not by their good works. For in that case, God's grace would not be what it really is–free and undeserved.*
>
> ROMANS 11:6 NEW LIVING TRANSLATION

Have you given grace lately?

Have you ever heard the saying, "Favor isn't fair?"

Well, it is fair. Favor comes with the covenant of being God's child. He covers us with grace because that's what He promised, and His promises never return void. Our works do not determine the bountiful blessings of God, nor are we rewarded based on how long we've sat in life's waiting room. It's simple. God gives grace because He loves us, not because it's required.

As believers, we are to be diligent in seeking Him regardless of what happens. Grace is not reimbursement or payback for anything we have done; nor are we offering an exchange for services. Being humans, we lack stability, faith, and character, and yet, God still projects His favor on us. He chooses to cover us in His everlasting grace throughout our lives.

Often, we grab hold of grace and never let go. We use it as a comfortable blanket that keeps us warm when life's chill comes upon us. We act as if it is protection when we've sinned, and remove it when we judge others who do the same. God's faithfulness is our redemption that lets us know that we are no different from our neighbor, yet we treat each other as if we are superior. God does not give grace based on color, creed, or level of sin. We are all equal in His eyes.

Unfortunately, we fail to apply this same principle. We are blinded by someone's fall, and never look beyond their fault into their future. We hypocritically ridicule and refuse to give grace. Jesus said, "Let him without sin cast the first stone," because everyone is equal. We ought not to feed our pride with God's favor. We cannot continue to pick up God's promise and keep it for ourselves. Without the ability to pass on our blessings and bless others, we won't be fulfilled in life and actually want to live it. If we can't grant simple kindness to others, then we are living in a grace tunnel where we deem ourself the only one worthy of God's favor.

Grace is for everyone.

Our life objective is that we must follow God through Jesus Christ and apply His principles. Christ shows that grace must, in turn, be given to others. The grace that you give others flows from the abundance that God has given you. It is not due to your own strength or power. You must choose to keep servanthood first.

Take Action

Are you in a grace tunnel? Have you passed judgment on others and failed to provide favor? Your obligation is to bless others as God has blessed you. Ask God to forgive your self-seeking ways and change your heart to follow His principles.

12

Pure Heart

> *Blessed are the pure in heart, for they shall see God.*
>
> MATTHEW 5:8 ENGLISH STANDARD VERSION

What does your heart look like?

In this era of humanity, many falsify reality to soften their image.

People are hidden behind pretense until evidence reveals the truth. Eventually, what's on the inside will come out. The desperate desire of one's heart to fit in will never constitute the pleasure of being yourself. One truth that will always filter to the top is how much water you mix with your anointing oil.

As the saying goes, "Will the real you please stand up?" But the real question is, "Do we even want to see the real you?" Putting on a façade—pretending we have it all figured out and that we don't need God—will lead us to life's waiting room so quickly that it'll make our head spin. God must sculpt and mold our hearts, but He first must show us the person we've become. Now, it is our choice as to whether we take the next step. Recognizing the necessary changes is one thing, but doing the actual work is another.

The unfortunate mishap is that people fail to do the work. They are satisfied living the same way and getting the same result. Then they turn right around and say, "I don't know why people talk about me." Yes, you do. Let's see. You're mean, judgmental, selfish, and cold-hearted. However, you reiterate that you're a nice person. If you're as nice as you say, why must you tell everyone? A person never has to brag about their good qualities; others do that for them. People bear witness to who you truly are. If you must tell people how wonderful you are, then chances are you're not as wonderful as you say.

Get rid of the residue.

Let God help today. Our passion should be to have a pure heart with good intentions to do God's will and serve His people. Our minds can be transformed, and God can grant us understanding about areas in life we need to conquer. We have one goal: be better than we were yesterday.

Take Action

Is your heart pure? Reflect on your intentions and your attitude. Are you all about yourself, or are you all about serving God's people? Take an honest look in the mirror and ask God to give you a pure heart.

13

Your Intentions Need Attention

> *Walk in wisdom toward outsiders, making the best use of the time. Let your speech always be gracious, seasoned with salt, so that you may know how you ought to answer each person.*
>
> Colossians 4:5–6 English Standard Version

Why aren't you living in the moment?

The treasures of life are the moments that we continue to long for.

It's our everyday dreams that propel us to keep moving forward. Within the whirlwind of life, we tend to be laser-focused on our day-to-day duties. Whether you're a parent, spouse, or friend, life has a way of making you feel stagnant— yet time is still moving. We are wasting weeks, months, and years, with the best intentions but the least attention. We move daily with a vision that is blinded to the cares of others.

We encounter people, whether strangers or acquaintances, that need more than just a "Hello" or "Thank You." Although, we may pray to God to be used for His glory, our opportunity to impact anyone is given to us daily. We are no longer living in the moment or seizing the day. Our focus is getting through the day without any interruptions getting in our way. We focus on work, dinner, and children to name a few, but we need to expand our hearts and focus on being helpful, providing Spirit-led guidance, or just being a friend. We are losing opportunities day in and day out to talk to the waitress who is wondering how she's going to pay her bills, the Senior Executive who comes to work with scars on her face every other day, the mailman that has cancer, or the mother whose child has run away. We may not know their situation, but everyone is going through something.

A few weeks ago, my husband, little sister, and I were eating inside a fast food restaurant. As we were eating, I looked out the window and saw a white van pull up. A woman got out of the van yelling and screaming. The driver, a man, then got out of the car and talked to her. I could not hear the conversation, but she wanted nothing to do with him. She got her groceries out of the car, dropped his cell phone on the pavement on purpose, and sat at a picnic table. The van then circled the block. She got back in the van, and they would argue again, only to have her get back out of the vehicle. This was an obvious domestic dispute, but she needed some attention.

When we were leaving, I had every chance to approach her, to not only calm her down, but give her someone she could talk to for just a moment. That moment was nothing but an opportunity to be intentional about doing God's will—help those in need. Did I make the right decision? No, I did not. I was concerned about eating and getting to a volleyball tournament on time. I could've spared two minutes. I mistakenly validated my decision, but it could've changed her life.

Be intentional.

Now I think about her daily. What if? What if I would have taken the time to talk to her? What if I could have introduced her to Christ? This has made me recognize that we have to reach out to people in the moment. We need to be more aware of our surroundings. If we become more aware, we'll be able to see that whoever we encounter may need our attention. Wake up from just going through the motions! Today is your day to be used by God to change each person you meet.

Take Action

Ask the Holy Spirit to guide you to meet people that need an encounter with Jesus Christ. Pray for guidance for the words you should speak. Be intentional today, and every day.

14

Purposeful Living

> *And we know that all things work together for good to those who love God, to those who are the called according to His purpose.*

ROMANS 8:28 NEW KING JAMES VERSION

Are you waiting on purpose or are you waiting on PURPOSE?

There are two definitions of waiting on purpose.

One is waiting on your calling, and the other is wasting time by being stagnant. Purpose and procrastination are opposites that battle to restrain or regain your destiny. Whether you're trying to get to your purpose or failing to see there is something more in store for you, God has a purpose for you. The disappointment of waiting for your purpose to be revealed can leave you fragmented and confused. The coldness of never reaching your potential will leave you frozen.

How do you find your purpose? Or better yet, when are you ready for your purpose? Early on, I would ask God what I was supposed to do on this earth. My heart yearned for something of substance. When I finally took the path of healing from my past and obeyed God by writing *Invisible Dad*, it finally clicked. My purpose was revealed. My purpose is to help others conquer their unbearable pasts so that they too can walk in their purpose and propel in the future.

In my book, *Invisible Dad*, I discuss my challenges of growing up as a fatherless daughter. I ran from my feelings until I finally had a breakdown. The revelation that my past of anger, rejection, and depression were keeping me from stepping into my purpose stopped me in my tracks. What could I have done differently? What was my purpose activator? My past and my future would crash like water on the seashore, but not until I stepped into my healing was my purpose revealed.

Healing reveals your purpose.

And how did I *step into my healing*? It took ten years of fighting myself. Ten years of bitterness. Ten years of enduring pain after pain. Ten years of traveling the road most traveled. Just like the Israelites, how much time would I have saved if I weren't lost in the wilderness? The principle is not that I could fast track the waiting; the principle is I needed to pinpoint the problem and pursue healing. Since I ran from it and didn't want to stand in my truth, the outcome would be wandering around in a desolate place longer than necessary. I had it all wrong. I was not waiting for God to reveal my purpose; I was waiting on myself to stop being stagnant.

Are you wondering why your purpose has not been revealed? My question to you is, "Have you healed from your past?" If you can heal from your pain and become whole, then you can, in turn, help others to do the same. Wholeness is the undergirding of purposeful living and thriving in your future. It's time to step into your purpose, but first, you must heal from your past.

Take Action

Take the first step toward healing by standing in your truth. Write down the actions you are going to take to walk in wholeness.

15

Full with Nothing to Pour

> *He has made everything beautiful in its time. Also, he has put eternity into man's heart, yet so that he cannot find out what God has done from the beginning to the end.*

ECCLESIASTES 3:11 ENGLISH STANDARD VERSION

What are you withholding?

The woes of society can overshadow our lives to the point of exhaustion.

The saying goes, "You can't pour from an empty cup." I found this to be true on several occasions. I was trying to give, but I was giving out of a dry, empty place. My lack would not profit anyone's gain. When you give and give, you must be replenished.

As I progressed in my relationship with God, I thought the same thing was occurring—I was dry. But once I stepped back to gauge my life, this time it was different. *I was full.* This was not a similar scenario where I hid to recover from having the life pulled out of me. My cup wasn't empty; in fact, it was filled to the brim. How could this be? I needed to be submerged in God's unwavering love, power, confidence, and timing. Until God was ready, I retained the boundaries that would cement my position. I was full with nothing to pour.

> *Your butterfly moment is coming.*

I sought familiarity, but if I looked deeper, the abnormality was evident. Elevation will always come with new sacrificial ties and constant self-reflection. I needed to learn the necessity of waiting on God. It was not that I didn't want to pour. God was prohibiting me from giving myself to others through His powerful constraint. I was like a caterpillar transitioning from its beginning stage of life. I needed inner work that took dedication and progress. The cocoon was for me and God. I was growing behind the curtain of the world's eye.

Challenges of this life can gouge your perspective. Even though I was unseen and pressing toward fulfilling my growth track, I wasn't sure how to handle the withholding. I was so used to helping others, that it was abnormal to focus on spiritual growth. God led me to withdraw in order to increase, but the devil would have me think that my value to God was not worthy of the obedience. Contrary to the devil's belief, this was not true. If the suppression was going to work out for my good, I had to grasp that the assignment was mine. Of course, I wanted to take it into my own hands, but I truly had nothing to give. My heart needed to be open to hearing the unknown and recharging in wisdom, discernment, and authority.

One thing was clear. When I emerged, I would never be the same. God was saving me for such a time as this—when wisdom crosses with discernment and intersects with hearing His voice. Although the cocoon process would challenge me to look in the mirror and grow to my next level, I would become a butterfly with beautiful wings to prove that the sacrifice was well worth the wait.

Take Action

Are you full but constrained? Know that this is a time for growth and reflection. God is making you a butterfly. Store up all you can by keeping a journal. Your release date is drawing near.

16

Money vs. Mission

 *I don't care about my own life. The most important thing is that I complete my mission, the work that the Lord Jesus gave me—to tell people the Good News about God's grace.*

ACTS 20:24 NEW CENTURY VERSION

Have you checked your motives lately?

As people of God, we each have a mission.

Our missions may be different, but the goal remains the same. We all are to add to the kingdom and spread the good news of Jesus Christ, and with that goal, our missions are intertwined. As we run toward the mark, sometimes we forget to check our motive. We tend to get caught up doing our mission the world's way—the worst way. Often, we're focused on the financial outcome of the mission, instead of the reason we are doing the mission in the first place.

As a woman that is full of persistence, I was on the move exploring what God wanted for my future. I had reached a point while working in corporate America where I said, "There has to be more to life than this." Working for a dollar will leave you broke, but working for the mission will leave you woke. Jesus says it like this, "But stay awake at all times, praying that you may have strength to escape all these things that are going to take place, and to stand before the Son of Man." Luke 21: 36 ESV. When you start itching for something more, you know it's time to proceed to the next step in life's journey, your purpose.

After writing *Invisible Dad*, I finally found my purpose: *helping others overcome their painful past so that they can thrive in the future.* Although I wasn't aware of what it would entail, I did know I was standing in my calling. As Steve Harvey says, "A career is what you're paid for. Your calling is what you're made for." I knew I wasn't made to help people with their banking. I was made to help people change their lives. As I explored what that meant, all I heard was *sell, sell, sell,* and *money, money, money.* Everywhere I looked, it was the money that was the motive, not the mission. People were pushing money as the objective, when *it was subjective to the mission.*

God asked me a simple question during this time: "Is your motive the money or the mission?" This question would pierce my heart. He showed me that it is critical to evaluate my motive in order to substantiate my mission. Even though I had not made any steps towards my calling yet, God didn't want me to fall. Of course, everyone wants to make money, which is definitely not an issue. It's God's principle that we should be blessed abundantly. The overwhelming problem is that the incentive of building strong relationships to help fulfill the mission is not greater than selling something to someone just to make money and "hope they change." If our motive is the mission, then we will surely get the money. But when our motive is the money, we will lose sight of the mission and miss our opportunity to adhere to our calling.

Same God. Same Goal. Different Mission.

In the Bible, the love of money motivated Judas. He walked with Jesus for over three years. Three years of hearing God's principles. Three years of seeing miracle after miracle. Three years of smelling the sweet aroma of freedom from the hypocritical conviction of the Pharisees and Sadducees. Yet, he betrayed Jesus Christ, God's only begotten Son, for thirty pieces of silver because his motive was greed. Even when guilt set in and he wanted to give the money back, it was too late. This story shows you that you can walk with Jesus Christ and still miss your mission because you have the wrong motive. The motive of money killed Judas' mission. Don't let it do the same to you. Ask yourself, "How much is one changed life worth?" The amount of money you can make should never be your motive when changing lives is your mission and God is your motivation.

Take Action

Heart Check! Check your motivation for your mission. Why do you do the things you do? Will it benefit the kingdom?

17

Cipher Invasive Visions

For still the vision awaits its appointed time; it hastens to the end – it will not lie. If it seems slow, wait for it; it will surely come; it will not delay.

HABAKKUK 2:3 ENGLISH STANDARD VERSION

What's your vision?

Have you ever had a vision?

It flashes in your mind and then leaves. You are unsure what to think or believe. You question whether it's real or a figment of your imagination. Invasive visions happen all the time, but the key is to understand who sent them. God is the powerful force behind helping His people be better servants for His glory, but Satan only comes to kill, steal, and destroy.

There are two types of visions, those that Satan puts in your mind to keep you in bondage, and those God gives you as direction for your present or a depiction of your future. There is a distinct difference. Satan's vision will leave you repeatedly rehearsing the woes of your past. He will keep you bound and rehearsing images and situations in your life that cannot be changed. Satan prompts you to always look backward. God's visions are the exact opposite. They will help you on your path today and give you hope and evidence of what will happen in the future. You must be able to tell the difference, or you'll subject yourself to the waiting room of life based on false evidence.

Cast down the visions of Satan. Don't give them space to run rampant in your mind. You don't want to subject yourself to such torture only to add more chains to your life. Satan will try to steal, kill, and destroy your future by bringing back the disappointment of your former days. There's only one way to overcome Satan's visions–focus on God. He will remove those visions from your mind and break the chains of your past.

God's vision will offer much more. I remember in 2009 when I was presented with the opportunity to do something different. During my graduate years, I could choose to study abroad. I always

> *Sunrise or sunset your vision.*

wanted to go to China and understand the culture, so God gave me the vision to move forward. This was a great time to take advantage of my intense desire to travel abroad. Once I started to tell people what I wanted to do, I heard it all–how I shouldn't go because there is "a lot happening over there," and how, "It's not the United States, and you need to keep yourself on U.S. soil." There was no concrete evidence as to why I shouldn't go. It was all hearsay and fear.

I was persistent and went on the trip. It was one of the best experiences of my life. The Chinese culture's perspective of time has impacted me to this day. What I learned was impeccable, but what if I had let others dictate the vision that God had given me? I would not have had the experience. *Your vision is worth moving forward.* You don't have to withdraw because someone else has never traveled the journey. Take the leap. All you need is you and God, and He will execute it perfectly.

Never let people's emotions affect yours. Your vision was never given to them. It's yours. You must protect it at all cost. Your expectations of others understanding your path will only leave you to question if you had a vision in the first place. Just because they may not have your vision, doesn't mean you should abandon your vision. You are being called higher, but until you understand that everyone cannot handle what you have, you will be left without the fulfillment of your destiny.

Take Action

Do you have a vision that you're not quite sure of? First, determine if it is from your past, present or future. Once you have determined the source of the vision, you'll either need to cast it down or step into its fulfillment and protect it. Always carry out God's plan for your life.

18

Say Nothing, Gain Nothing

Truly, I say to you, whoever says to this mountain, 'Be taken up and thrown into the sea,' and does not doubt in his heart, but believes that what he says will come to pass, it will be done for him.

Mark 11:23 English Standard Version

Are you saying anything?

Do you remember how class participation was important in school?

The teacher would require you to raise your hand and add to the conversation, whether it be answering a question or stating your opinion. If you did not follow the rules, he/she would take note, and your grade would suffer. The rule itself was simple to follow and rendered great results, but for some reason, some students did not participate.

This lesson is not just for school; it's for life. God has given us promises throughout the Bible that will help us in life. These anchors are a depiction of His steadfast love and devotion to His people. They are the breadcrumbs that we follow to the Promised Land. We may not need all of them now, but we will need all of them during our lifetime. All the principles contain action, but the simplest principle is the one that only requires us to speak.

Speak things into existence.

In the Bible, Jesus said we should speak to a mountain for it to move. Speaking not only changes your situation, but it causes a shift. The mountain not only moves; you don't have to go through the trouble of climbing over it just to get to the other side. Action from you will result in action on your behalf. You must say something to gain what you're looking for. The trenches are only the trenches until you begin to speak something different. If you are calling the trenches treasures, then based on God's principles, you will find treasures.

As children of God, our tongues are gouged as if Satan has removed our ability to speak things into existence. This is not the case. You are empowered to wreak havoc and wreck reality. Say it! Speak blessings over your life. Speak to life's mountains and say, "Be thou cast into the sea." Speak to spiritual bondage and say, "You're not getting me nor my future generations." Stand in the truth and feel empowered to know that God is your support, and He will not let you be overtaken by broken promises, life-sucking people, and miserable circumstances. Come out of the cage and be free to have what you say!

Let me be clear; this principle should not be confused with speaking to the waiting room of life just to get out of it. It does not work that way. This principle is strictly for Satan who imposes his force to trouble your life with obstacles by trying to kill, steal, and destroy you. You must distinguish between the devil's ploy and God's plan. There's a difference. One will make you better, and the other will make you bitter. However, God will work *everything* out for your good if you believe.

Take Action

Research God's promises. Get sticky notes and write a promise on each of them. Start with 10. Put these stickies everywhere–refrigerator, bathroom, bedroom, car, on the back of your cell phone, and on your desk at work. Read them aloud daily. They will stand as a constant reminder of Whose you are and Whom you serve.

19

Don't Let Your Bell Ring Over Dry Land

 *But as for you, be strong and do not give up, for your work will be rewarded.*

2 CHRONICLES 15:7 NEW INTERNATIONAL VERSION

Have you given up?

My husband and I were watching a Mixed Martial Arts (MMA) fight recently.

The competitors were not equal in stature. One was overwhelmingly larger than the other. After the action had begun, the effort began to show. The smaller opponent would throw a punch, and sometimes it would miss, and sometimes it wouldn't. The larger opponent would not connect all the time either, but when he did, you could imagine how much harder the impact.

The smaller guy had to have more endurance and be twice as vigilant as his opponent. He did not let the fear of what he saw overtake his belief. He had to keep in mind that it only takes one hit to defeat his obstacle. He knew that the bigger they are, the harder they fall. Round after round the bell would ring, but he never tapped out. Finally, the officials rang the last bell, and the fight was over.

In life, sometimes, you are the smaller opponent taking blows that have knocked you across life's waiting room. You've had a knock down drag out with the devil himself, and it appears

Stay in the fight.

the fight is not worth the energy, effort, or mind numbing pain. Your focus is to get through the fight and get out of the waiting room of life, but you'll find out that you must fight your way out. Fear and vulnerability may set in, but you have faith in God and an obligation to yourself to keep getting back up. You can be beaten to your core, looking to be revitalized, but when you tag in God, He'll always show up.

God guarantees that the fight will be for your benefit. 1 Timothy 6:12 says, "Fight the good fight of faith." A fight is only *good* if you win. Even though the success may not be immediate, we continue to complain, lack faith and never make it to the rich Promised Land. Instead of waiting on God to ring the bell when the fight is over, we take matters into our own hands and ring the bell ourselves. Why would we ring the bell when we're still standing on dry land? Don't tap out when the fight is fixed. It may be tough, but it's not over. It'll never be over until God says it's over. Get what you came here for–the reward. Stay in hot pursuit of God's best. Tag Him into your fight, and you will win every time.

Take Action

Have you stopped fighting? Get back in the fight. God is ready to fight your battles, but not until you let Him into your situation. Tell God today that He is welcome into your circumstance. Ask the Holy Spirit to guide you through your next moves.

20

Sifting the Sitting

 *Now to Him who is able to do exceedingly abundantly above all that we ask or think, according to the power that works in us.*

EPHESIANS 3:20 NEW KING JAMES VERSION

What's your position?

In Luke 22:31, Jesus makes Peter aware that Satan has asked for him,

so that he may sift him as wheat. Satan is not the only one who sifts. God has a way of allowing the enemy to come a little closer so that He can sift our sitting. Many times, God permits the testing because He wants us to move in faith. In response, we sit on our situation with the expectation that God will stir up the atmosphere and make things magically appear.

Our illusion is incorrect. The key to exiting the waiting room of life is not sitting. Waiting and *actively* waiting are two separate things. We must actively wait to get to the next level. This is not the time to let life happen. It's also not a "let the chips fall where they may" situation. We must take advantage of the power that God has put in us and the Holy Spirit who is there to guide us. God is sifting our sitting so that our promise can be manifested. It's time to get up! We won't receive until we first become active.

The specific position does not move God, but failing to take Him at His word will leave us stagnant. Our minds are inundated with what we can see, and it hinders what we believe. We will never see the miracles of God because we fail to stand in the faith that His power is more than sufficient. We must stand on the word of God and pray for help to increase our diligence and knowledge of His promises. The power is not in the promise itself; it is in Who said it. God's preeminence is your omnipotence.

As a newlywed, God would sift my sitting. Rather quickly, my husband and I decided to build a home. We looked at neighborhood after neighborhood, lot after lot. Finally, we found a lot that we loved, but we were quickly told that the requirements for the house would cause us to exceed our spending limit. This was an exclusive neighborhood with very large homes. We accepted the devastating news and began looking again. There was nothing available that we liked, so we decided to settle on a lot. While moving forward with the floor plans, the lot we loved was still on my mind. I talked to my husband about it, and He said, "We can't afford it." Here's the problem, when we settle, we will never see the miracle. We did not like the lot we had, and I refused to move forward with something that we did not want.

When you get sick and tired of being pushed around in life, change is bound to occur. I asked myself, "Why do I say the word of God, but don't apply it when the miracle looks like it cannot be done?" I was fed up with the usual. Others were saying how the neighborhood was exclusive and how the land had too many requirements so we could not afford it. I saw God work financial miracles for many other people. Why could I not have the same thing? I was determined to build a house on that lot despite others' opinions. We decided to take a leap of faith and cancel the purchase of the current lot.

Among many things that Pastor Rod Parsley taught me, one thing stood out during this time: The atmosphere of expectancy is the breeding ground for miracles. It was time for a miracle because I was expecting more this time. The first step was to put a financial offering in church specifically for this miracle. Seeds will always reap a harvest if you plant them in fertile ground. Second, while my husband was working, I went to the vacant land with my mother, anointed it with oil, and declared in Jesus' name that this would be ours. Lastly, I sat back and waited. I could do nothing else. It was time for God to step in.

As soon as you get up, the blessings will come down.

Take note that you must be diligent with who accompanies you during this time. I did not need someone who was half sold on the vision God gave me, nor a person that does not have enough faith to believe that God could and would work this out for our good. Fifteen years earlier, my mom walked around a vacant lot seven times claiming the victory in Jesus' name. God made the miracle happen for her, and it was now my turn.

I wish I could tell you that we moved forward with building our house on that lot, but that wouldn't be true. After meeting with several builders, it really left us with no choice but to give up. But, I wasn't giving up without a fight. I went back to the lot, got out of my car, and walked the land by myself. "God what do You want me to do? I've prayed for it, put a seed on it, walked around it, anointed it, what else?!" At that moment, I turned around and started to walk back towards my car. As I looked down, I found a corner of a dollar on the ground. I heard God speak, "Trust me with your dollar." I said, "Okay," and left. I had no idea what would happen next.

Shortly after we gave up our favorite lot, we started looking again. We found a brand-new subdivision, and the downtown view was gorgeous. After we made all the changes we wanted, it still was way too expensive. Our realtor reached out to the builder and gave them a price of how much we were willing to pay. Needless to say, that $500 seed came back to us one-hundred-fold. The blessing is that we're building a great home for our family. The better news is that I learned to trust God no matter what it looks like. I was persistent enough to take God at His word and actively wait.

Take Action

Why are you sitting? It's time to shake things up a bit. God is not a respecter of persons. What He has done for my husband and I, He can do for you. Get up and put motion behind God's manual.

21

Rejuvenating Faith

> *Count it all joy, my brothers, when you meet trials of various kinds, for you know that the testing of your faith produces steadfastness.*
>
> James 1:2–3 English Standard Version

Do you have faith?

There's a secret to increasing your stamina and courage throughout life.

It takes hard work, but most of all, it takes the waiting room. You not only have to stay in the race, but you must also get to the finish line. By working through trials and tribulations, there's a certain burst of fulfillment that is given when you exit. It takes time, but the outcome is a transformation that everyone needs.

The waiting builds endurance, but the trial increases your faith. Faith is your rejuvenator to keep holding on to the truth of God's word because you have seen it work firsthand. You cannot reach beyond your present situation and believe that things will work out for your good if you've never had to wait. The story of one's testimony does not constitute the substitution of yours. Everyone must have their own trial for faith to be their anchor and saving grace. Otherwise, the lack of wisdom and influx of supposed authority will make one think that they have the authority to be their own Savior.

Life is fine in the beginning until you get in the thick of it. I've tried to get myself out of countless situations just to escape the waiting room of life. To my disadvantage, I would fail every time. I tried to heal alone but ended up running from my problems. I tried to be bold on my own but ended up shrinking in fear to make others feel worthwhile. I tried to feel free on my own, but the overshadowing of Satan would break me every time. For every circumstance and life situation I've encountered, the truth still holds—I can't make it on my own. In my own abilities, I fail. I am unable to increase my own faith and increase my steadfastness to move to the next level.

Like a fresh water spring, faith is refreshing.

Through Christ, by faith, we have our being, which challenges us to reach higher and dig deeper into understanding. The overcoming of trials is the sweet refreshing that can only come out of the fiery furnace of affliction. For if you never had a battle, how would you ever know that God could solve them? If your faith was never tested, then how would you know if you had faith? The overwhelming truth is that it would be impossible.

It is difficult to consider our trials useful; yet we must trust in the One that is greater than us, the One that the wind and waves obey, the One that can create a human being out of clay. Most of all, we must increase our faith in something greater—God. He relieves the obligation of having to get it right. It's a sweet, refreshing gift that allows us to believe, and trust in Him

Take Action

Often, we fail to have faith in God because we refuse to live by His timetable. We must cast our opinions aside and believe that the One that knows all, also knows that we need Him to show up in our situation. Increase your faith today by writing down every problem God has solved for you and your family. Reflect on your list, and you'll obtain rejuvenated faith that He'll do it again.

About the Author

While many choose to wallow in self-pity when life doesn't deal them a full deck of cards, she chose to convert her pain into a greater purpose. Growing up with the absence of her biological father, Candice Crear, is committed to leading people worldwide from the road of adversity to the highway of wholeness. As the international best-selling author of Invisible Dad, Invisible God, I'm Waiting, and From Fatherless to Fearless, she gives readers the tangible tools they need to move forward. She challenges them to confront their true story, despite anger and rejection. Candice seeks to strengthen, revitalize, and reenergize many who have grown weary in life through healing and empowerment. This International Book Awards finalist is there with you in the trenches, and teaches you how to navigate the journey of being fearless. She offers tangible nuggets of inspiration to carry readers to their destiny.

As the visionary of the B.R.I.D.G.E.™ technique, Candice encourages others to pinpoint their pain and use it to pivot them to purpose fulfillment. She motivates women to enjoy the journey, even in the midst of life's stumbling blocks. In addition to holding a Bachelor of Science from Winston-Salem State University and a Master of Business Administration from Xavier University, Candice is also a Certified Project Manager. She resides with her husband in Cincinnati, Ohio.

For more information on Candice Crear, visit www.CandiceCrear.com.

www.ingramcontent.com/pod-product-compliance
Lightning Source LLC
Chambersburg PA
CBHW080412300426
44113CB00015B/2496